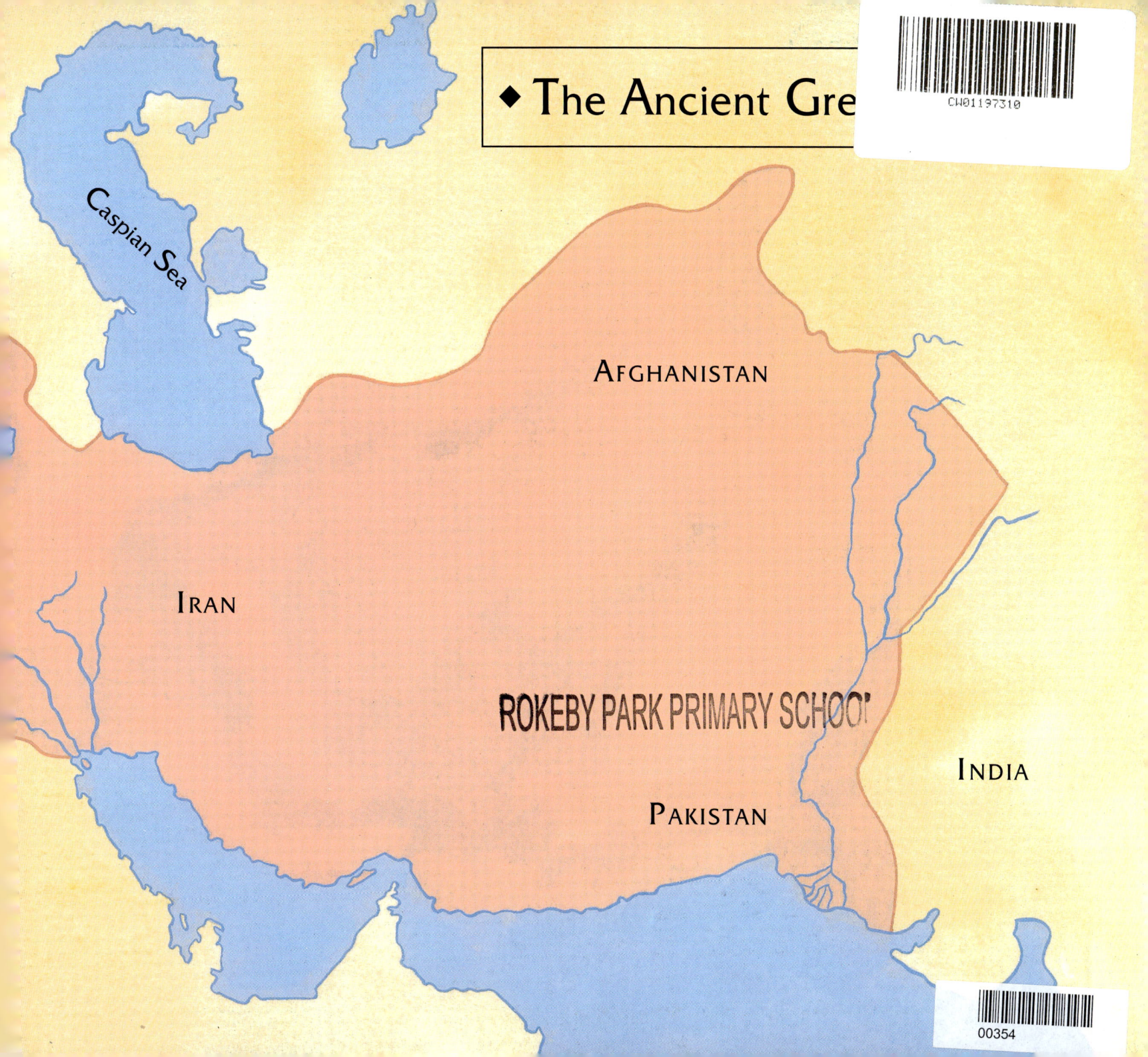

◆ The Ancient Gre

Caspian Sea

Afghanistan

Iran

ROKEBY PARK PRIMARY SCHOOL

India

Pakistan

First published in Great Britain in 1999
by Macdonald Young Books,
an imprint of Wayland Publishers Ltd

Macdonald Young Books
61 Western Road
Hove
East Sussex
BN3 1JD

Find Macdonald Young Books on the
internet at: http://www.myb.co.uk

Text © James Riordan 1999
Illustrations © Nilesh Mistry 1999

Commissioning Editor: Dereen Taylor
Editor: Rosie Nixon
Designer: Miriam Yarrien

© Macdonald Young Books 1999

Riordan, James
Hercules and the golden apples. - (Magical myths)
1.Hercules (Roman mythology) - Juvenile literature
I.Title II.Mistry, Nilesh
398.2'2'0937

ISBN 0 7500 2757 6

All rights reserved

Printed in Hong Kong

HERCULES
and
The Golden Apples

◆

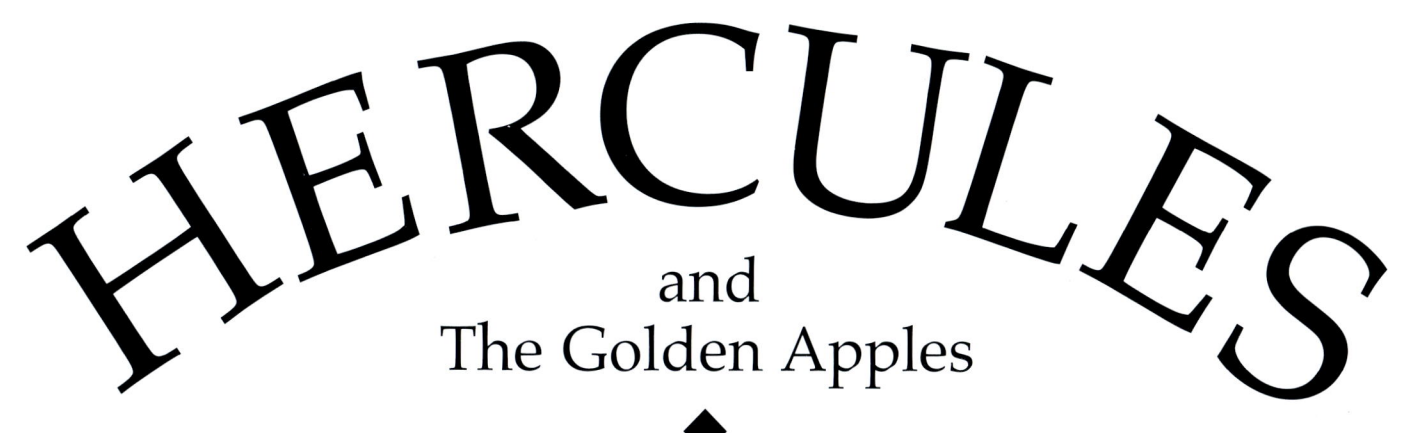

Written by James Riordan
Illustrated by Nilesh Mistry

MACDONALD YOUNG BOOKS

INTRODUCTION

The Ancient Greeks lived in cities on the islands and coasts of the Mediterranean Sea. Under Alexander the Great, the Greeks conquered a vast empire, stretching to the borders of India. Tales of heroes first told in Greece spread across this empire.

No hero was more famous than Hercules – known in Greek as Heracles. He was called Hercules by the Romans who also told his story. Today we remember Hercules, as he is most commonly known, by calling a very difficult task 'herculean'.

Hercules's father was Zeus, father of the gods. When Hercules was born, Zeus called him after his wife, Hera

(Heracles means 'Glory to Hera'). But Hera was furious, for the child's mother, a woman called Alcmene, was not a god. Hera was determined that bad luck should follow Hercules like a shadow.

In one fit of madness caused by Hera, Hercules killed his own family. To pay for this crime, he agreed to undertake twelve 'impossible' tasks – one of which is described in this book.

Loved by the gods, Hercules was the strongest, bravest man on Earth. He was tall and broad-shouldered, with dark, flowing hair and a gaze like raging fire. When angered, this superhuman could destroy everything in his path.

One of Hercules's twelve tasks was to seek three golden apples from the Garden of the Hesperides…

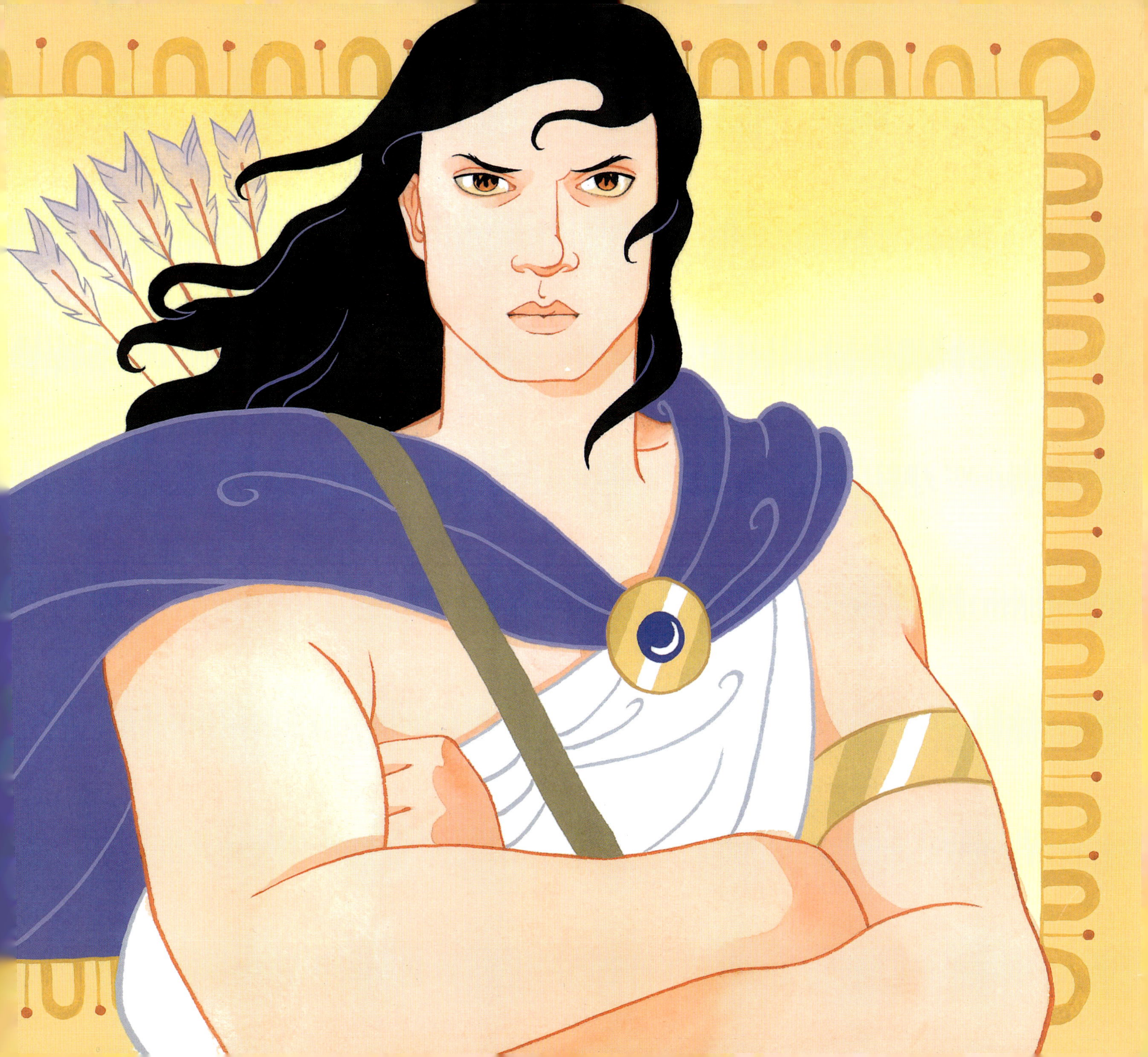

Now, the golden apple tree was a wedding gift from Zeus to his wife Hera. A scaly hundred-headed serpent guarded the tree. Its coils wound about the trunk and it kept one eye open all the time – even when it slept.

The sleepless beast would crush any thief in its coils and poison him with its fangs.

As if Hercules's task was not hard enough, another obstacle stood in his way. Only the gods knew where the apples grew. All that anyone else knew was that they were looked after by the three daughters of the giant Atlas. They alone could pick apples from the tree.

Hercules wandered through many lands in search of the golden apple tree. But no one could help him. Finally, as he was walking one day beside a distant sea, he came upon three water nymphs – lovely young women with sea-green eyes and skin the colour of moonlight.

'Can you tell me where the golden apple tree grows?' asked Hercules.

Charmed by the mighty hero, they replied in chorus, 'No, but our father can. Nereus knows all things past and present. But you must seize him tight, for he will change shape to avoid sharing his secrets.'

Hercules splashed through the water until he came to the sleeping Nereus covered in seaweed. On finding himself in the hero's strong grasp, Nereus at once turned himself into seawater – but Hercules clenched his fists tightly to stop the water running through his fingers.

Straight away, Nereus became a fiery flame that burned his captor's hands – yet still Hercules clung on. Next, Nereus changed into a raging lion that would have torn apart a normal man.

But not Hercules. After a brief struggle, he was about to choke the beast when Nereus gave up the fight and took his usual shape.

The old man of the sea sighed and told Hercules all he wished to know.

'The Garden of the Hesperides lies on the slopes of Mount Atlas in Africa. To reach it you must first kill the serpent that guards the tree. Even if you do, however, you will not be able to pick the fruit yourself. Only Atlas's daughters can do that.'

Once more Hercules set out on a long journey. He crossed burning sands and rocky mountains, steaming swamps and icy waters. At last he arrived in the foothills of Mount Atlas where he found the garden with the golden apple tree.

As Hercules came near, the serpent's hundred heads turned towards him and a hundred tongues flicked out. The evil beast came sliding across the grass to crush him in its coils.

In no time at all, a perfectly fired poisoned arrow through the heart put an end to the scaly guardian of the tree.

Remembering Nereus's words, Hercules climbed to the top of the mountain to find the giant Atlas. Poor Atlas had the task of carrying the heavens upon his back.

When Hercules
explained why he had come,
Atlas agreed to help.
 'I will have my daughters
pick three apples,' he said.
'But you will have to hold this
globe while I go to find them.'

As Hercules took the heavens upon his shoulders, Atlas set off down the mountain.

He was soon back with the precious fruit. Hercules was impatient to be on his way, but Atlas had no wish to lose his freedom. The longer Hercules carried the globe, the more reluctant Atlas was to take it back.

Hercules would have to outsmart the giant.

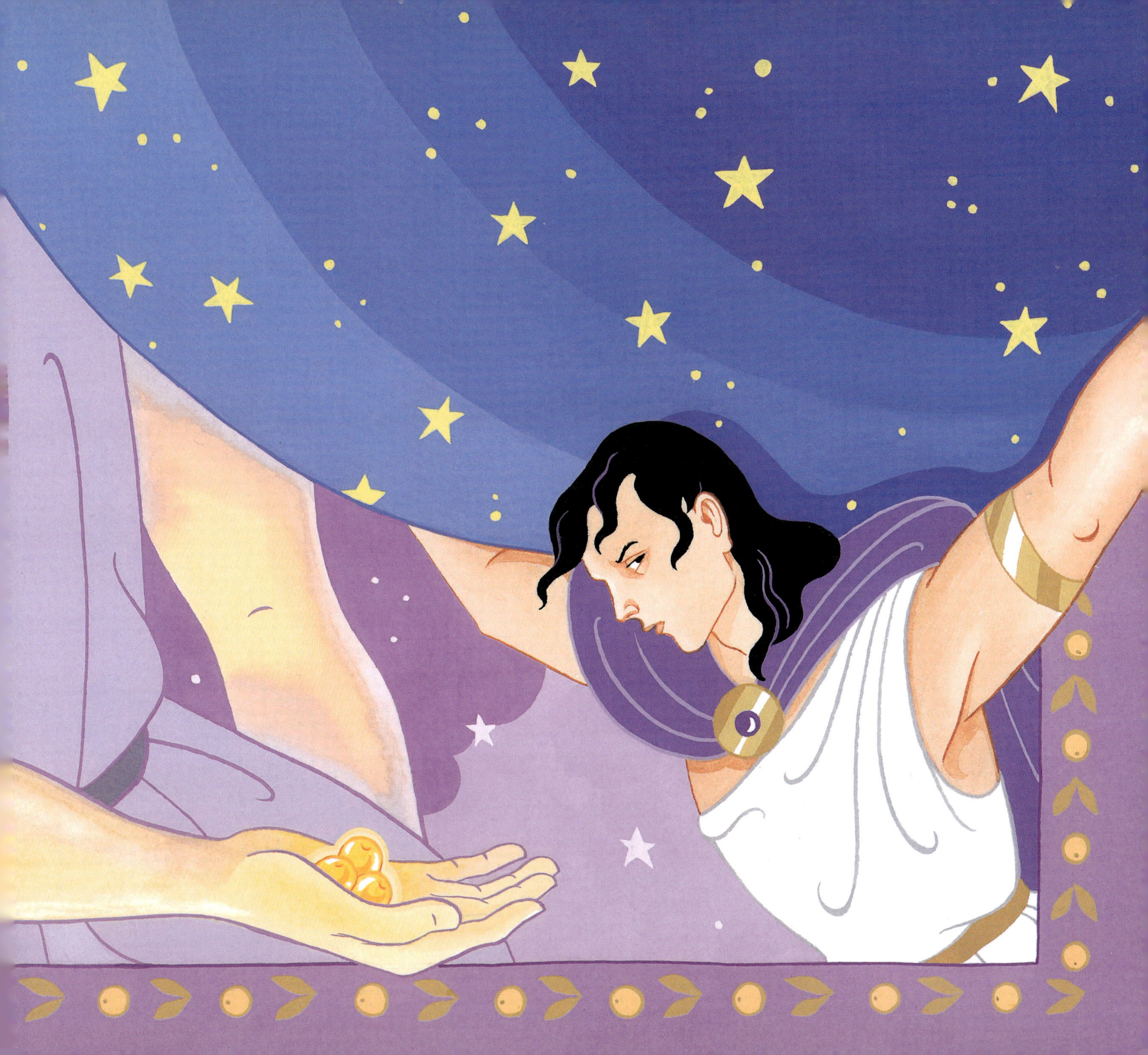

'Atlas,' he said, 'I fear the globe is slipping off my back. Take it for a moment while I bend my shoulders to hold it safely.'

As Atlas crouched down to take the strain of the heavens upon his back, Hercules breathed a sigh of relief. He was now free to escape with the golden apples.

Quickly, he stood up and hurried off down the mountain.

'Come back, come back,' yelled Atlas.
But Hercules did not give a backward glance.
Happily, he returned home with his prize.

This time Hercules had beaten Hera.

ITALY

GREECE

Black Sea

Mediterranean Sea

TURKEY

CRETE

CYPRUS

SYRIA

IRAQ

EGYPT

ARABIA

Red Sea

N

Ancient Greek Empire
(Around 325BC, as conquered by Alexander the Great, one of the world's most famous generals.)

Mount Olympus